JOSE ESTRADA

Denver Travel guide

Discover All top essential attractions, Restaurants & Hikes in Denver.

First edition

This book was professionally typeset on Reedsy.
Find out more at reedsy.com

Contents

1

Introduction

Welcome to Denver Travel Guide ! Thank you for purchasing my small travel guide. My name is Jose Estrada and My goal with this travel guide is to have you visit, in a short span of time, All of Denver's top attractions. Please note, Some of Denver attractions are seasonal and depending on the time of your visit they might be closed. As well as for when you're in your hotel room deciding what to eat.Or even maybe making up one early morning wanting to take a hike into the mountains and not knowing the best trails to take, Well I got you!

A small Introduction about myself, I have lived in Denver Colorado My whole life. I have visited every single attraction and even some hidden gems. I am 21 years old, but I do a lot of traveling in Denver, Such as going up to Lakewood, Colorado springs, Golden, Bloomfield. All considered to be part of my travel guide. That is why I decided to write this as I have been able to take my family to these attractions and had a good time.

This book will not give you all the details there is to know about Denver Colorado. My travel guide is mainly for a small trip of about 1 week. Around ten attractions, ten Restaurants. Some are just my personal recommendation as you know, it is better coming from a person who has actually been to the attraction or restaurant.

What you can expect is a small brief description unlike travel guides that list thousands of attractions for you to visit in a 2 day trip. Know that we have that out of the way let jump right into what you're looking for!

Pre-Planning —

When thinking of flying out to visit Denver, For family, Friends or even for fun. This is the average amount you will need to have a comfortable stay.

The Average daily cost to be in Denver is roughly $174 a day.

A week in Denver alone would be $ 1220
   A week in Denver as a couple would be $2440

Now let's move on to where to stay.

The average hotel cost is $139.00. I have experience in hotels, and depending on the day you come as well as the time of the year the rate can be higher or lower. For example: in summer it is peak season for hotels, Especially if you try to get a hotel; near the airport. The rate went up like crazy.

What I have seen in Denver is most people like to stay In hotels, Such as

Marriott, Hyatt, Hilton because they offer rewards programs and can be very beneficial to people who travel a lot.

Downtown is a very beautiful place to stay. Such an amazing place to be as well./ If you want a mountain view you can stay in places like cherry creek. That way you get a good view. As well as drive up to golden/Lakewood to get an amazing mountain view!

As far as AirBNB , The average price is around $137.00. Both hotels and AirBNB have a very similar rate. This would just depend on how you feel. Some people are more comfortable in a hotel with more people as others prefer renting a Airbnb for a more quiet place.

Now the third part that brings you the whole trip together is rental car or uber.

Rental cars have gone up in price but you can rent one from almost anywhere. Now as the generations have evolved they have come up with better ways of renting cars such as toro. They are a website where you can rent cars on a budget and they are good cars. They do have a mileage expense but it ends up being cheaper then most either rental cars. In my experience I rented a ford fusion for $49 a day and used it for about 4 days and it was mainly my work car and I only paid roughly $220 at the end. I was shocked as I have rented cars before and I had paid over $200 a day.

Now as far as uber/Lyft goes, It has been proven that now with a spike in demand it has gone up to .40 per minutiae around the world. It is always better to compare rates online for as far as you're going if it is close the average is about $10. My suggestion is to rent a car on toro if you decide to use apps like uber or lyft. You can create a free account and usually your first ride is free.

Now that we know the average cost of being in Denver aside from the hotel and car expenses, let's look at our attractions and restaurants.

2

Top Attractions

- Red rocks Park and Amphitheater (Live Music)

R ed rocks is such a beautiful place to go for a hike on top of being a great attraction! It has a full blown arena for you to go into and listen to live music. There are some free shows once in a while but even if you pay it is worth it. With such an amazing view, live music and some cold beer!

Hours of operation are:
  April - October: 7am-7pm
  November - March: 8am - 4 pm

Cost: $$$

Address: 18300 W Alameda Pkwy , Morrison Co 80465

- Denver Museum of nature and science

The Denver Museum of nature and science is such an amazing place to go! Especially if you have kiddos. This is a once of a kind place, from its space odyssey exhibit to its dinosaur exhibit. Show how the years passed and the meteor hit earth wiping out all dinosaurs. There is also a health part for kids to play and learn if they are healthy. As a huge 3 story high museum. The bonus part is that sometimes they have extra exhibits, such as "live dinosaurs" or Egyptian pharaohs. Another small bonus is that they have an IMAX theater that is always changing going from showing you how dinosaurs got wiped off the face of plaster earth. To show how global warming is affecting the Earth.

Hours of Operation:
    Saturday - Thursday: 9am-5pm
    Fridays - 9am-9pm

Cost: $$

Address : 2001 Colorado blvd , Denver Co 80205

- Denver Botanic Gardens

Denver Botanical Gardens is a very beautiful place to go to take photos with family. Or any event such as a wedding. It has inside and outside gardens, With a walk through water garden that is a must see! As beautiful as it is, it does contain over 43 gardens. Waterfalls as well! During the winter they do specials such as winter wonderland, or light shows.

Hours of Operation:
  Monday & Wednesday: 9am-2pm
  Every other day: 9am-8pm

Cost: $$

Address: 1007 York Street, Denver, Colorado

- The Denver Zoo

The Denver zoo is notorious for its wildlife. It has everything for a family to have an exciting time. Going around inn exhibits such as lions, Grizzly bears, Turtles, alligators and pythons. There is also a show of penguins, Which is also seasonal as the penguins are not always out. They also have a seasonal thing which is called the Denver zoo lights, it is such a beautiful sight to see. This is offered in December near christmas.

Hours of operation;
  Everyday : 10am-5pm

Cost: $$

Address: 2300 Steele st, Denver Co 80205

- Downtown Denver

16th street mall is located in downtown Denver and is a very beautiful place. During christmas and new years there is a huge tree right outside of 16 st mall and is so beautiful. Another thing is everywhere around 16 st mall is restaurant, more stores, Such as candy stores for the kiddos! Once you take a stroll through the 16th street mall on both ends you will be able to see some of the modern sky-scrapers. An attraction here is also the IMAX theater.

If you go to 16th street Mall and are already in the area of downtown it is a good idea to also go visit the state capitol. It is located in Civic center park, So on top of going over to visit this monument you will be able to go take a walk around the park and see other buildings such as modern sky-scrappers.

House of operations:
   Open 24 hours although the stores can vary

Cost: $$$

Address: 16th st mall , Denver co 80202

These are the top 5 Attractions from Denver, I hope you enjoy them!

3

Amusement parks

- Elitch Garden theme and water park

This is personally a favorite one for me! This amusement park has both water park and an amusement park at once. This would be considered a whole day out. You can start off in the water park shower and change in their locker rooms, then head to the amusement park to end the day. They even have a kiddy land for all the kids! On top of all of these great attractions they also have carnival-like games to win prizes. Yes, They do also have a food court, as well as small stands all over the park. Even on the water park side they have a full blown out bar, With all types of drinks. This is sadly a seasonal amusement park and is usually just in summer time. This is famous for the ride called the twister and it is one of the most popular rides in the whole park. Another thing i love about this park is personally the fact that during the summer if you buy a Elitch garden cup for 19.99 you get .99 refills the whole summer which is such a steal when you go a lot. They do offer season passes if you're here all summer, and you buy it for around 79.99 and if you go more than twice it is completely worth it! And an added bonus is you get 50% off food.

Hours of Operations:
   Monday - Friday: 10:30am-6pm
   Saturday: 10:30am-9pm
   Sunday: 10:30am - 8pm

Address: 2000 Elitch cir, Denver co 80204

- Water World

For hot weather like the one we experience here in Denver during the summer, Water world is the place to go! It is a full blown water park,

With its huge pool and waterslides and fun for all ages. There are even dining options here at waterworld.

Hours Of operation:
  Monday - Thursday : 10AM-5PM
  Friday - Sunday : 10AM-6PM

Address: 8801 N Pecos St , federal Heights co 80260

- Lakeside Amusement Park

Lakeside is very similar to the Elitch garden theme and water park. This is an older amusement park as it was built in 1908 and is more of a carnival looking amusement park. It makes it more fun, As it gives the oldies vibes.

Hours Of Operation:
  Monday, Wednesday , Thursday : 7AM-10PM
  Tuesday: Closed
  Friday - Saturday: 7AM-11:30PM
  Sunday: 2PM-10PM

Address: 4601 Sheridan Blvd , Denver co 80212
  These are the top 3 Amusement parks and I hope you enjoy your trip here!

BONUS:

- Gaylord Hotel & Resort

This is a Hotel. If you get to have a reservation here it is a spectacular hotel. This is the best place in Denver to stay as it has a full out pool , Slides Lazy river and a kids area as well. I love how the set up at this property is. The Inside has a full out food court as well. Not to mention they have treasure hunts around the hotel for kids to play and win prizes. The staff is great and all hotel rooms have an amazing view. When you drive up to this hotel you will see how massive it is. It Has a small Golf course, Basketball court , and Tennis court. This is the spot for a relaxing vacation.

This is open 24 Hours!!!!
Address: 6700 N Gaylord Rockies Blvd Aurora Co 80019

4

Restaurants

• Corinne Restaurant

This restaurant is located right inside the Meridian / AC hotel. A good place to stay as well if you decide to be in the downtown area. This is rated as the #1 restaurant in denver. With over 750 reviews all 5 stars! Offering both breakfast and dinner this is the spot.

Hours of Operation:
   Monday - Friday: 6:30AM - 11PM
   Saturday - Sunday : 7AM-2PM - 5PM-10PM

Address: 1455 California St , Denver co 80202

- 54thirthy rooftop

This is the second restaurant located in the Meridian/ AC hotel. The only difference is this is on their rooftop! With a great downtown view, and a spectacular bar. Rated at 4.5 stars. This is a great spot to end the night!

Hours of Operations:
  Monday - Wednesday : 4PM-11PM
  Thursday: 4PM-12AM
  Friday - Saturday: 1PM-12AM
  Sunday 1PM-11PM

Address: 1475 California st , Denver co 80202

- Hiro

Now if you're like me you love buffets! Hiro has 2 sides, A hot pot side and a buffet side. Both are extremely good. The buffet side is japanese/Chinese food. For thoses who don't know what a hot pot is, it is When you order a soap and bring it to you or you choose your topping , meats, Veggies etc, And everything is cooked in the soap. My favorite is adding dumplings to be steamed. This is a very good place to take the family as its food is really good.

Hours of Operation
  Monday - Friday : 11AM-3PM - 4PM - 9:30PM
  Saturday- Sunday : 11AM-9PM

Address: 2797 S Parker Road , Aurora co 80014

• Juicy Seafood

Now, I am adding this for the seafood lovers. This is the spot. Has amazing king crab legs. They have huge seafood trays. If you're looking for just something small they got you too, They sell bags with your choice of sauce and seafood. Their sauce is Mild , hot , Lemonpepper or mixed. I personally always get mixed. Great interior looking like a ship/cabin. With a live lobster tank for you to see as well. Great customer service here!

Hours Of operations:
    Monday - Friday : 11AM-10PM
    Saturday- Sunday: 11AM-11PM

Address: 2727 S Parker Rd, Aurora co 80014

• Fogo De chao

This has to be the best place to go to have smoked fresh steak! To explain better, This is All you can eat. Salads , and steak. Amazing food, the only catch is, it is very pricey! If you get the chance I would Highly Highly recommend going here.

Hours of Operation:
    Everyday 11AM-9PM

Address:1513 Wynkoop St Denver

I hope you get to go to at least one of these restaurants!

5

Denver Hikes

- Wild Basin in rocky mountain national park

This hike has a beautiful view. About every 3 miles there is a spectacular view, if you decide to do the full trip it is 12 miles round trip and you will see some amazing waterfalls. Such as calypso cascade

Distance: .5-12+ Miles
   About 90 min from Denver

Address: Allenspark Co 80510

Chautauqua park in boulder

This is a very nice trail as it contains more than a dozen different trails. This is probably one of the best trail systems and is located in downtown boulder.

Distance: .5 - 5.5 Miles
  About 40 Min from Denver

Address: Baseline Rd & 9th St , Boulder Co 80302

- Staunton state park - best waterfall near denver

This is a great place as the lake is a good place for fishing. As well as a good spot for a picnic during your hike. This is also a good place for mountain rock Climbing and mountain biking. If you take this trail you will end up seeing one of the best waterfalls!

Distance: 2 - 11 Miles
  About 40 Min from denver
  Address: 12102 S Elk Creek Rd, Pine Co 80470

- Rocky mountain National Park

If you're lucky you might see some vision up here. I have personally been here and ran into some vision. It is such a beautiful experience and depending on how you take this hike there can be different outcomes but every trail is beautiful. This is better when you have a rental car as it is a good drive up. On this hike you will pass 4 mountains and 4 waterfalls iof youtube takes the whole hike. Going up here they offer a map of the park so you can navigate and go any way you wish. Please note that Dogs are not allowed here.

Distance: .5-10 miles + more trail option available
   About 2 hours from denver (if you take I-70 straight)

- Red rocks

As one of the top attractions, It is also a top place to go for a hike. This is a beautiful hike up if you buy tickets to a concert i would suggest going early and go for a hike! Here you can go from the bottom on a trail that will take you up to the Amphitheater. With a loop trail that will take you to a waterfall.

Distance: 1-7 Miles
   About 25 Miles from denver

Address: 18300 W Alameda Pkwy , Morrison Co 80465

- Waterton canyon trail

This is a great place for a Hike. This is a great spot for a picnic with the family all around. As well this is a beautiful place to see the wildlife. Due to the bighorn sheep who live here it is a trail where no dogs are allowed.

Distance : 1-13 Miles
  About 35 min from denver

Address: 11300 Waterton Rd, Littleton

- Castle wood Canyon state park

Castle wood canyon is hidden behind castle rock. You can explore as there are old dam ruins. It is a sight to see. This park is very popular for rock climbing.

Distance: 1-4 Miles with other options
  About 50 min from Denver

Address: 2989 S Hwy 83 , Frank town

- Devil's head Lookout trail

This is a small hike, But it delivers a spectacular moment. The moment is due to the view you receive. This hike is popular for the view as you can see hundreds of miles of land.

Distance: 2.8 Miles round trip
   About one hour and a half from Denver

Address: 6518 S Rampart Range Rd

• White Ranch Loop Hike - Foothills

This trail is located just outside of the city and located in golden co. It is a small loop in golden that gives a good view of the city, NAd even looks better during sunsets. This is the final Hike i am adding to these 10 hikes. I hope that you enjoy your hike!

Distance: 4 Miles
   About 40 min from Denver Co

Address: 25373 Belcher Hill road, Golden Co 80403

Hope you enjoy the hike!

6

Shopping centers

I know a lot of you come here to shop! As an added bonus I will add the top Shopping centers in Denver.

- Colorado Mills

This is the best mall in Denver Colorado. It is a huge 1 floor story mall that is constantly adding new things. They recently added this car show where you go in and you get to look at the cars that were used in movies like Batman Forever, Fast and furious etc. This mall has a huge food court and arcades, and minigolf for kids. The other thing attached to this mall is Target, and burlington! This is a must go shopping. Located right by it is also an AMC theater!

Hours of Operation:
Monday - Saturday : 10AM-9PM
Sunday : 11AM-6PM
Address: 14500 W Colfax Ave, Lakewood Co 80401

- Flatiron Crossing

This is such a good mall, as it is located in broomfield it is in a good location that has a view. This is a mall where even across the street there is another shopping center and other food court. Filled with amazing things, Such as escape rooms to do with the family. They also have an outside playground for the kids, as well as an inside playground.

Hours Of operation:
   Monday - Saturday : 10AM-9PM
   Sunday : 11AM-6PM
   Address: 1 W Flatiron Crossing Dr , Broomfiled co 80021

- Denver Premium Outlets

This is an outside shopping center. It is full with your favorite brand outlets! Having a massive food court but with the option to make it like a small picnic since it is outside. It also has a new park for kids to play in. Since these are the outlets of Denver it is a place to go since there are always more deals at the outlets!

Hours Of Operations:
   Monday - Saturday : 10AM-8PM
   Sunday : 11AM-7PM
   Address: 13801 Grant St , Thornton co 80023

- Castle Rock Outlets

Adding this one for more outlets. This is very similar to the outlet of Denver; it is just located in Castle rock. It is also a very nice place with discount items!

Hours of Operation:
    Monday - Saturday : 10AM-9PM
    Sunday : 11AM-6PM
    Address: 5050 Factory Shops Blvd #437 , Castle rock Co 80108

• Cherry Creek Mall

Cherry Creek mall is in the heart of cherry creek and is such a well made mall. It is a two story building. Having issues with finding how to decor your house? They have a place fully decorated and you can purchase that is 5 stories high of just how rooms would look. This is a good mall, Although there is not very men clothing here it is more of a girly mall. Also inside the mall is having a AMC theater.

Hours Of operation:
    Monday - Saturday : 10AM-9PM
    Sunday : 11AM-6PM
    Address: 3000 E 1st Ave , Denver Co 80206

• Park Meadows mall

Parkmedows mall is in such a good area. Surrounding this mall is everything you need from In-n-out , krispy creme , Buffalo wild wings,

Everything! They even have a cheesecake factory in this mall! Aside from food it is also a 2 story building with so many different options. As well as ross near it. It also has a spirit halloween right behind it every time we are in the spooky season.

Hours of Operations:
   Monday - Saturday - 10AM-8PM
   Sunday - 11AM-6PM

Address: 8401 Park Meadows Center Dr. , lone tree co 80124

• Aurora Mall

Aurora mall has the most fashion. It is filled with good stores and I know you'll find something you like here! It also has a playground for the kids and an arcade and mini gold for them as well. Now they even built a rec center. There are also stores like burlington , ross, best buy etc. Right outside the food court entrance is Century 16 , a beautiful theater with reclining chairs! My favorite theater around!

Hours of Operation:
   Monday - Thursday - 11AM-8PM
   Friday - Saturday - 10AM-8PM
   Sunday - 12PM-6PM

Address: 14200 E Alameda Ave, Aurora Co 80012

Have fun Shopping!

7

Conclusion

Thank you so much for purchasing my small travel guide. There is way more to see in Denver than just this. Please leave a review and i can always do a bigger travel guide, Or a guide on moving to Denver Colorado!

Thank you and hope you enjoyed it!

8

Resources

Your Trip, B. (2021, May 4). *Denver travel cost - average price of a vacation to Denver: Food & Meal Budget, Daily & Weekly expenses*. Budget Your Trip. Retrieved August 11, 2022, from https://www.budgetyourtrip.com/united-states-of-america/denver

All The rooms. (2022). Average Airbnb Prices By City [2022] | AllTheRooms. Https://Www.Alltherooms.Com/Analytics/Average-Airbnb-Prices-by-City/. Retrieved November 8, 2022, from https://www.alltherooms.com/analytics/average-airbnb-prices-by-city/

All The rooms. (2022). Average Airbnb Prices By City [2022] | AllTheRooms. Https://Www.Alltherooms.Com/Analytics/Average-Airbnb-Prices-by-City/. Retrieved November 8, 2022, from https://www.alltherooms.com/analytics/average-airbnb-prices-by-city/

Law, L. (2021b, September 5). 16 Top-Rated Attractions & Things to Do in Denver, CO | PlanetWare. Https://Www.Planetware.Com/Tourist-Attractions-/Denver-Us-Co-d.Htm. Retrieved November 8, 2022, from https://www.planetware.com/tourist-attractions-/denver-us-co-d.htm

Trip Advisor. (2022). THE 10 BEST Restaurants in Denver - Updated August 2022 - Tripadvisor. Https://Www.Tripadvisor.Com/Restaurants-G33388-Denver_Colorado.Html. Retrieved November 8, 2021, from https://www.tripadvisor.com/Restaurants-g33388-Denver_Colorado.htm

Day Hikes Near Denver. (2020, June 22). Hikes Near Denver - Our Top 10 Favorite Hikes. Retrieved November 8, 2022, from https://dayhikesneardenver.com/top-10-hikes-near-denver/